HOW TO DRAW

W9-AWY-405

Nintendo®

GREATEST HEROES & VILLAINS

Written and Illustrated by Ron Zalme

SCHOLASTIC INC.

New York   Toronto   London   Auckland   Sydney   Mexico City   New Delhi   Hong Kong   Buenos Aires

ISBN-13: 978-0-439-91324-9
ISBN-10: 0-439-91324-1

Published by Scholastic Inc.
SCHOLASTIC and associated logos are trademarks and/or registered trademarks of Scholastic Inc.

11 10 9 8 7 6 5 4 3 2

7 8 9 10/0

Printed in the U.S.A.
First printing, January 2007

EVERYONE KNOWS THAT NINTENDO'S WORLD

of characters is fun for anyone, at any age, to play on game consoles and hand-helds ... but they're fun to draw as well!! In this step-by-step guide, you'll learn how to render all your favorite Nintendo heroes and villains! Beginning with a basic concept sketch to capture the movement of a figure in action, you'll use the fundamental shapes found in nature to construct your characters and bring your drawings to life.

THE FIRST STEP

an artist takes to begin a drawing is to look for the action lines. Action lines are just a few simple strokes of the pencil that represent the "flow" or direction of the pose of a figure. They may not necessarily need to conform to any of the actual shapes found within the figure, but they correspond to the "movement" within the figure – the way the body parts line up to give the figure a sense of dynamic motion.

The next step is to sketch the basic shapes that make up a character's body. All you can really draw on a piece of paper are two-dimensional flat shapes. Part of the magic of drawing is learning how to create the illusion of three-dimensional objects on your two-dimensional piece of paper. A circle is round and two-dimensional. Now imagine a real ball. It's also round, but it's three-dimensional, a real object. The trick to drawing believable characters is to create the illusion on paper that what you are looking at is three-dimensional. Every two-dimensional shape has a three-dimensional "partner." Simply by adding two crisscrossing dotted lines to the circle, you create the illusion of its three-dimensional partner, the sphere. Practice drawing two-dimensional shapes, then move on to the three-dimensional shapes like the cube, pyramid, etc. Once you've done that, you're ready to try drawing your first character.

Let's begin with the
MOST FAMOUS NINTENDO CHARACTER –

MARIO!

MARIO™

STEP ONE:
Begin with the two "action lines" to define the direction of the pose. The vertical line shows the body direction and center of gravity. The horizontal line reflects the arc of the shoulders and arms. Next, using basic circles and ovals, arrange the head and hands. Then sketch in the lines that show the positioning of the hips and legs and sketch in the shapes for feet.

STEP TWO:
Over your drawing, sketch in the basic shapes that define Mario's general body shape and features. Don't get wrapped up in any details yet... just block in the eyes, mouth, and nose and use simple shapes to indicate things like fingers and thumbs.

STEP THREE:
Now that Mario is taking shape, it's time to further define the figure and add details such as his fingers, mustache, and hat. Take particular care in rendering the eyes—there should be one oval each for the iris and pupil and one small circular highlight on the pupil.

STEP FOUR:
Now it's time to finish the drawing... erase the sketch lines you don't need and make the lines that look most like Mario bolder. Add the final touches such as intricate costume details and you're done!

2

4

WALUIGI™

STEP ONE:
Again, begin with the gray action lines to capture the pose. The lines show you how to place the angle of the head and to sketch in the hands and feet. Notice the small "crosshairs" that indicate where the eyes, nose, and mouth will line up.

STEP TWO:
Now start sketching basic shapes to fill out the body. Use tapered cylinders for the arm and leg shapes. The sphere on the hips helps to define the abdomen while also helping to properly locate the position of the legs.

STEP THREE:
Move on to the details and finalize the shapes for fingers, facial features, and costume design.

STEP FOUR:
Clean up your drawing and "tighten" up the rendering with nice bold pencil strokes. Finish any costume details you left out and Waluigi is ready to make trouble.

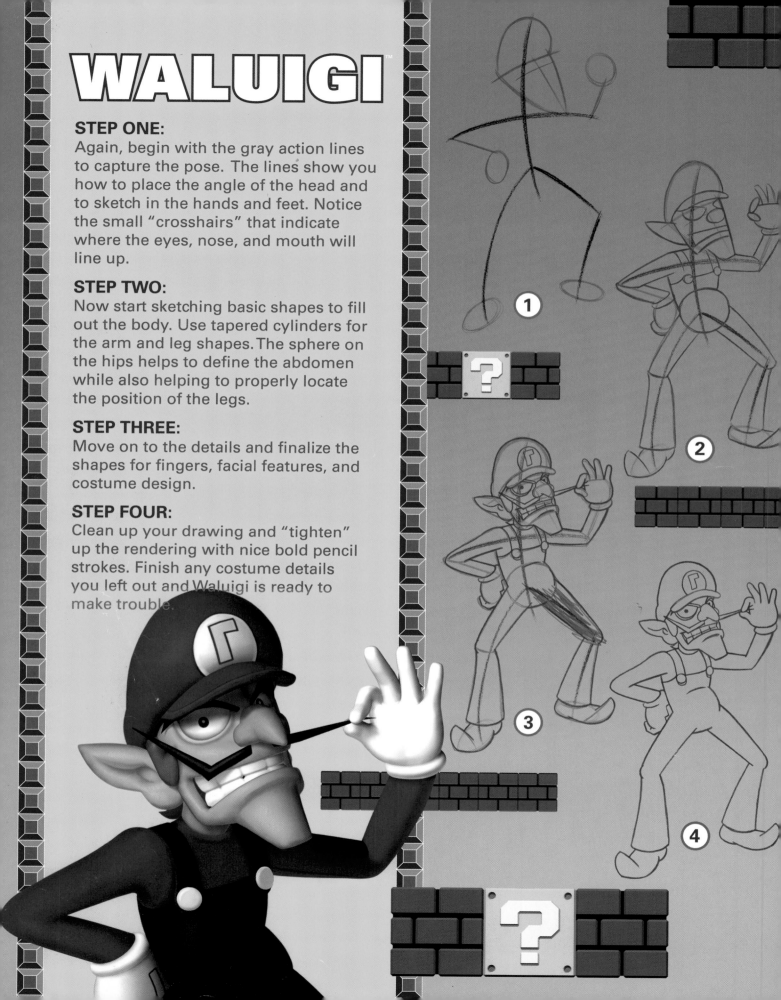

TOAD™

STEP ONE:
Sketch in the action lines and use large circles to indicate placement of the head, body, and extremities.

STEP TWO:
Sketch in the very large circle for the "mushroom cap" and use the crosshairs to place the eyes and mouth. Add vest and arm shapes and then refine the ovals used for the feet.

STEP THREE:
Add in the costume details and delineate the fingers to make complete hands.

STEP FOUR:
Erase your early construction lines and render the lines that best describe the figure so Toad can get back to the castle and help Princess Peach!

LUIGI™

STEP ONE:

Luigi is in a very active jumping pose, so keep your action lines lively! First, sketch in the action lines. Then add the oval head shape, the hands, and positioning of the hips, legs, and feet. Notice the "hip line" that helps give the character dimension.

STEP TWO:

Rough in the basic shapes to flesh out the character's body and remember to keep the drawing light and lively. A stiff-looking drawing will stifle the action of the pose. Notice how Luigi's right leg is bent behind him. An artist uses "perspective" to make a flat drawing look three-dimensional.

STEP THREE:

Now add greater detail to the facial features and costume. Notice how Luigi's expression adds to the excitement of the pose. Consider how the look of the pose would entirely change if you altered Luigi's expression and he were smiling or laughing!

STEP FOUR:

Finish your drawing by erasing unnecessary lines and developing the lines that best define Luigi. Now he can get back to helping his brother, Mario! Well, as soon as he lands anyway.

②

④

PRINCESS PEACH

STEP ONE:

One challenge for an artist is to think past the clutter of a pose – the costumes and accessories – and imagine the actual figure that is often hidden. Even though the princess is costumed in a long gown, make sure the action lines follow the flow of the figure beneath and consider where the feet would be positioned if you could see them.

STEP TWO:

Overlay the necessary basic shapes to fill out her body. Don't try to draw in all her hair at once. Start by concentrating on the top part and add the rest later.

STEP THREE:

Now draw in the details and pay particular attention to the way her fingers are clasped and her gown is flowing. Draw the facial features with as few lines as possible to keep the princess looking attractive – the fewer the lines, the prettier she will look.

STEP FOUR:

Now it's time to clean up the drawing and complete the princess. Keep your linework smooth and precise and she'll look as delicate and sweet as a Peach!

BOWSER

STEP ONE:
Draw the crisscrossed action lines and start to block in the rough shapes that construct Bowser's body. Begin the head shape with a softened triangle. This can be made by grouping several ovals together.

STEP TWO:
With his armored shell, Bowser needs a large amount of room to accommodate his form. Be generous when sketching in his basic body shapes so that he'll maintain his massive proportions.

STEP THREE:
Now that the basic construction is done, you can start putting in all the details like teeth, spikes, and armor. Don't forget to add his tail!

STEP FOUR:
Clean up your drawing and look for any details you might have missed. Did you get the claws? The spike on the end of the tail? Now Bowser's ready for action!

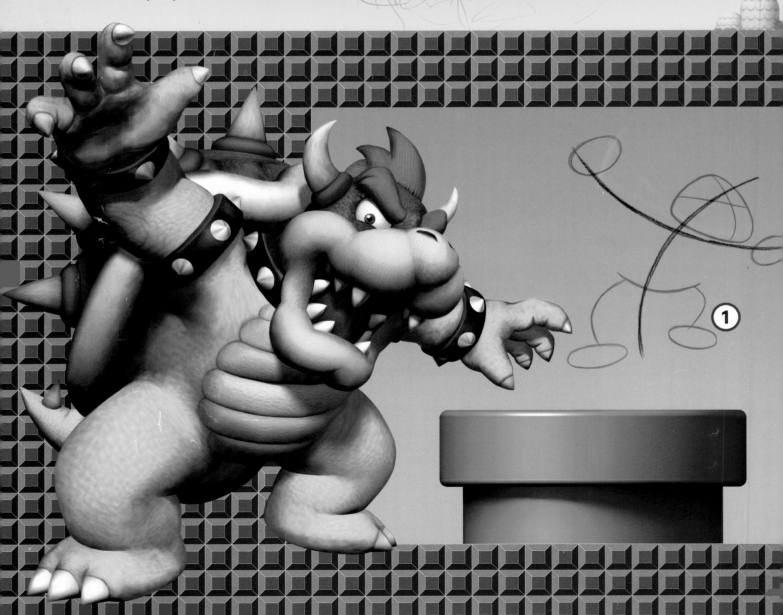

1

YOSHI

STEP ONE:
For Yoshi, draw the vertical action line as a gentle backwards "S" curve. That'll help you get the alignment of the character's body correct. Then add in the shape for the head and the positioning for the hips and legs. Next, sketch the ovals for the feet and hands.

STEP TWO:
Along the established action lines, sketch the rough shapes to build the body structure. Use a full circle to form Yoshi's muzzle. A circle guide or compass is a useful tool for this.

STEP THREE:
Refine your drawing by adding the details as shown. Study the example carefully and then make the alterations and additions as necessary. Don't be afraid to use your eraser!

STEP FOUR:
Now that all the details have been completed, you can finish your drawing and add the final touches. What do you suppose Yoshi has in the egg this time?

1

3

2

4

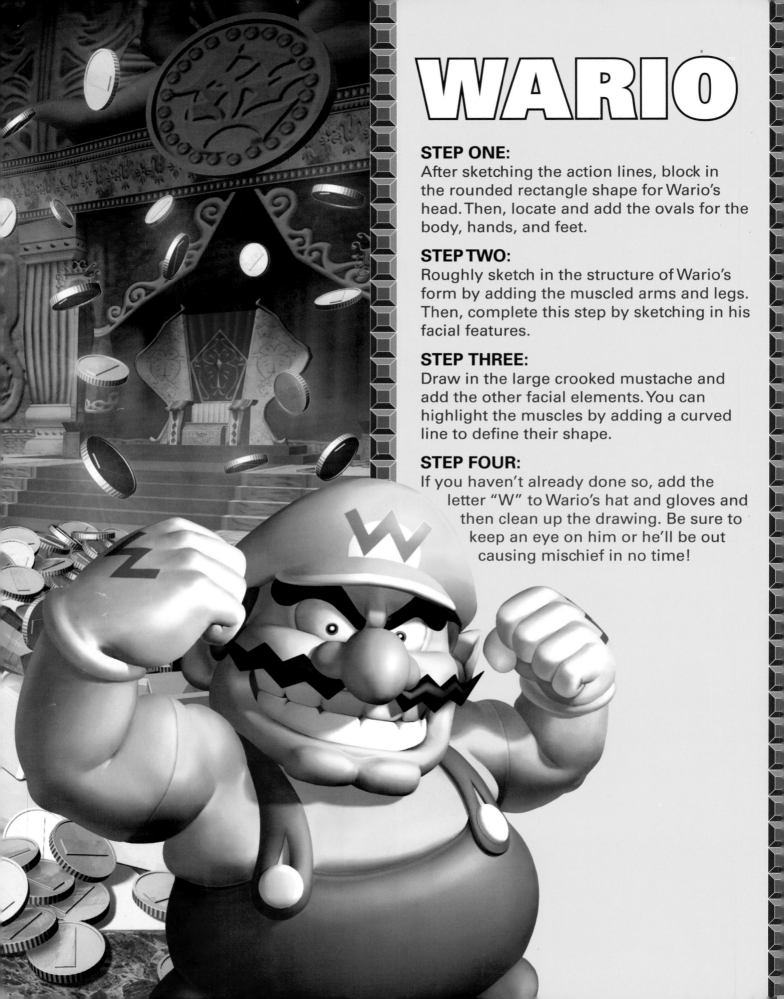

WARIO

STEP ONE:
After sketching the action lines, block in the rounded rectangle shape for Wario's head. Then, locate and add the ovals for the body, hands, and feet.

STEP TWO:
Roughly sketch in the structure of Wario's form by adding the muscled arms and legs. Then, complete this step by sketching in his facial features.

STEP THREE:
Draw in the large crooked mustache and add the other facial elements. You can highlight the muscles by adding a curved line to define their shape.

STEP FOUR:
If you haven't already done so, add the letter "W" to Wario's hat and gloves and then clean up the drawing. Be sure to keep an eye on him or he'll be out causing mischief in no time!

DONKEY KONG

STEP ONE:

The trick to this pose is to exaggerate the action and fool the eye into thinking that Donkey Kong's fist is really coming toward the viewer! To do this, the artist uses a method of perspective called "foreshortening." That means that the part closest to the viewer is drawn really large, allowing the rest of the figure to quickly recede behind it in perspective. When sketching his legs pay particular attention to the way his legs cross.

STEP TWO:

Over the sweeping action lines of the first step, sketch in the shapes that will block in the figure. Because the fingers of his hand are so large, you can sketch them in individually but don't get too concerned over their detail yet.

STEP THREE:

Render the features to capture DK's scowl and add his necktie! Another new art effect that you haven't encountered in previous drawings is the fur! Since fur is a texture, render its fluffiness with swirled wisps. You might want to practice some different "fur effects" on a separate sheet until you're happy with the style.

STEP FOUR:

Clean up your drawing and Donkey Kong is ready to rumble! Try applying the fore-shortening effect on some of your other characters. Remember to build them through the same steps and you should get interesting results!

2

3

4

1

2

3

4

DIDDY KONG®

STEP ONE:

Create the dynamic sweeping action lines, add the large oval for Diddy's head and the crosshairs for the facial features. Next, draw lines for the arms and finish by placing the ovals for the hands and feet. Just as with Donkey Kong, pay attention to the position of the hips and how the legs cross over each other.

STEP TWO:

Sketch in the partial circle for Diddy's muzzle and then locate the other facial features around it. Fill out the rest of the body by aligning your shapes along the paths you set up in Step One. A simple line for the tail is sufficient for now.

STEP THREE:

Now, add in the details for the body and face. Draw the details for his shirt as well. Note that the only fur texture to be concerned with is the "cuffs" that appear by his hands and feet.

STEP FOUR:

Did you notice the foreshortening on the raised foot? Did you manage it correctly? If so, you're ready to finalize your drawing and clean up the sketch lines. Diddy's done!

FOX

STEP ONE:
Even a static pose such as this one can have a lot of "life" to it if you keep your action lines full of energy. Sketch the action lines first and then position the hips, legs, and arms. Even though you can't see Fox's hands in this position, use a circle to indicate their approximate position.

STEP TWO:
Use the crosshairs to locate and place Fox's facial features and then sketch in the forms to build the body structure. The overlapping arms are easier to do if you draw all the structures lightly first and then focus on the shapes from foreground to background.

STEP THREE:
Now, add in all the details such as the features and costume elements. Also draw his headset and don't forget his tail!

STEP FOUR:
Now clean up the drawing and darken the lines you like. Check for any costume details you might have missed and Fox McCloud is ready to take on the universe!

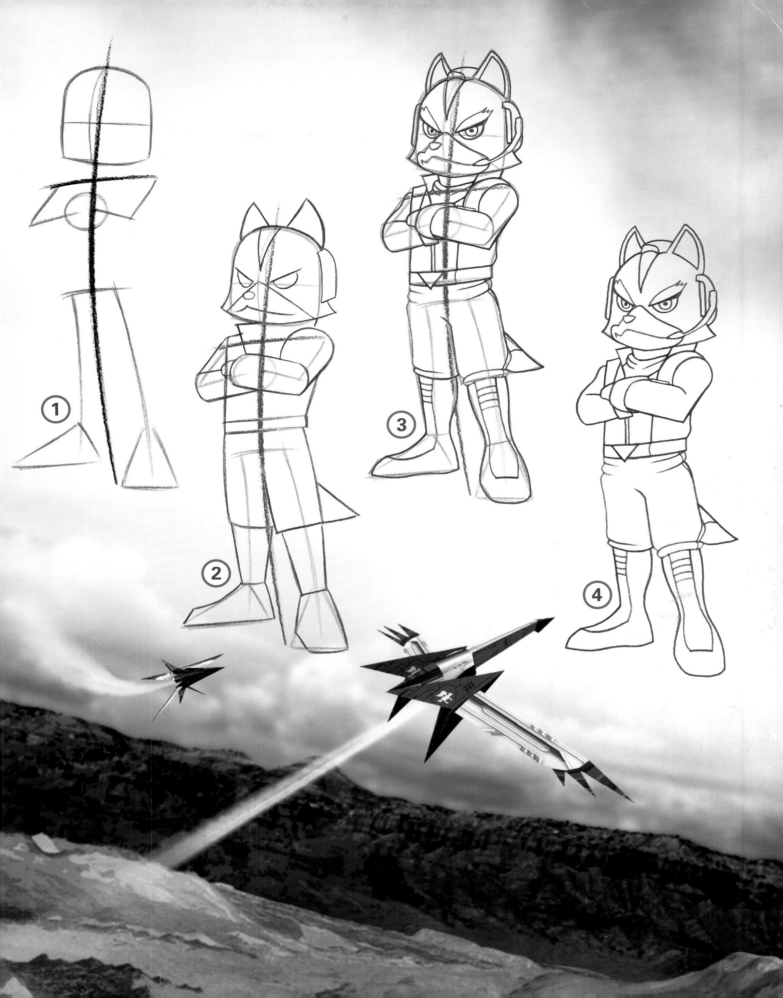

SLIPPY™

STEP ONE:
Begin with your action lines and then draw in the basic shapes of his figure. Once again, a circle guide or compass would be handy for rendering those circles. You can also trace around any circular object that is the same size such as a coin or a drinking glass.

STEP TWO:
Construct the rest of the shapes needed to structure the body, but keep your sketching light until you're sure the shapes are positioned correctly.

STEP THREE:
Render the remaining shapes and add in the features of Slippy's face and costume. Pay particular attention to the eyes and the pattern on his suit.

STEP FOUR:
Finalize your drawing with the erase-and-enhance technique you've already used and then double-check your drawing for any details you might've missed. Slippy's ready for his next invention!

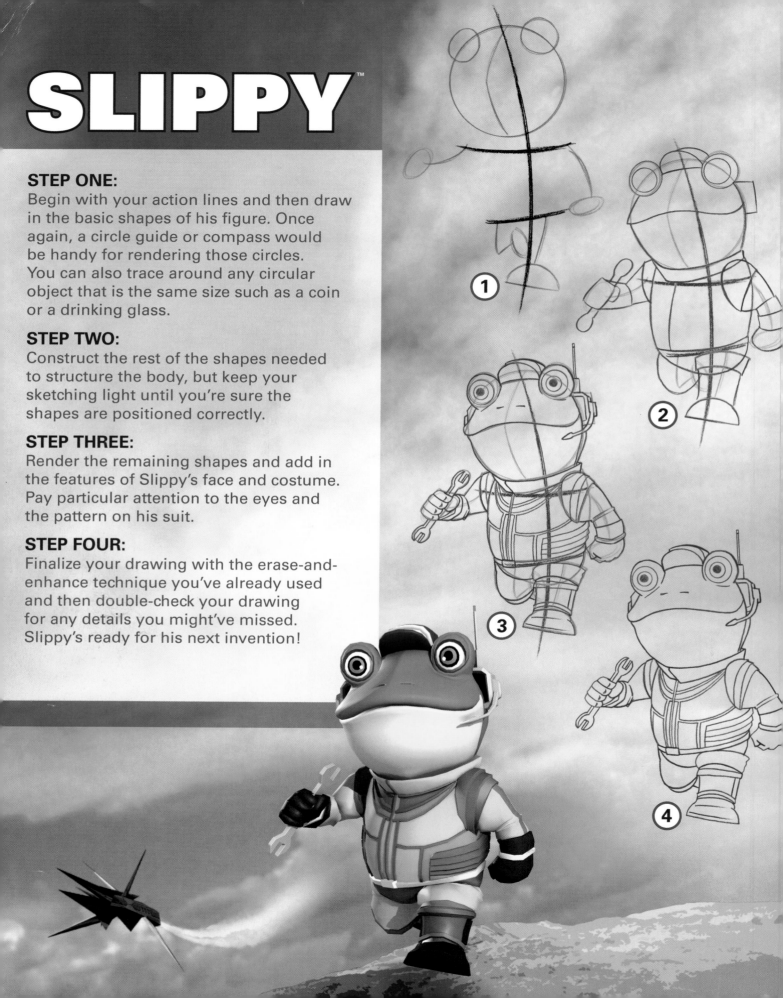

FALCO ™

STEP ONE:
Sketch in your action lines and add the correct shapes, ovals, and triangles to begin building your character.

STEP TWO:
Layer the shapes that will construct Falco's body. He is standing in a sideways pose, so all his left side appendages need to be in the foreground and overlap the rest of the body.

STEP THREE:
Sketch in the features and details. Carefully construct the eye and beak to maintain Falco's birdlike appearance.

STEP FOUR:
Tighten up your drawing by choosing the lines you want to keep and the ones you can erase. Finish off the costume details and Star Fox's best pilot is ready to soar!

1

2

3

4

SAMUS ARAN

STEP ONE:
The action lines are a simple cross, but keep the lines curved and lively! Sketch in the shapes and keep in mind the foreshortening on the arm-cannon (though not as severe as Donkey Kong).

STEP TWO:
Rough in the shapes for the body. It might be best to consider working from the front of the figure to the rear, allowing each element to overlap as you go.

STEP THREE:
There are a lot of complex costume elements to deal with. Begin by sketching them in as groups of larger shapes and refine them by adding the finer detail. Use your eraser as necessary!

STEP FOUR:
Lastly, clean up your drawing and compare and correct the costume details if needed. With Samus on your side, you're safe from any stray Metroids!

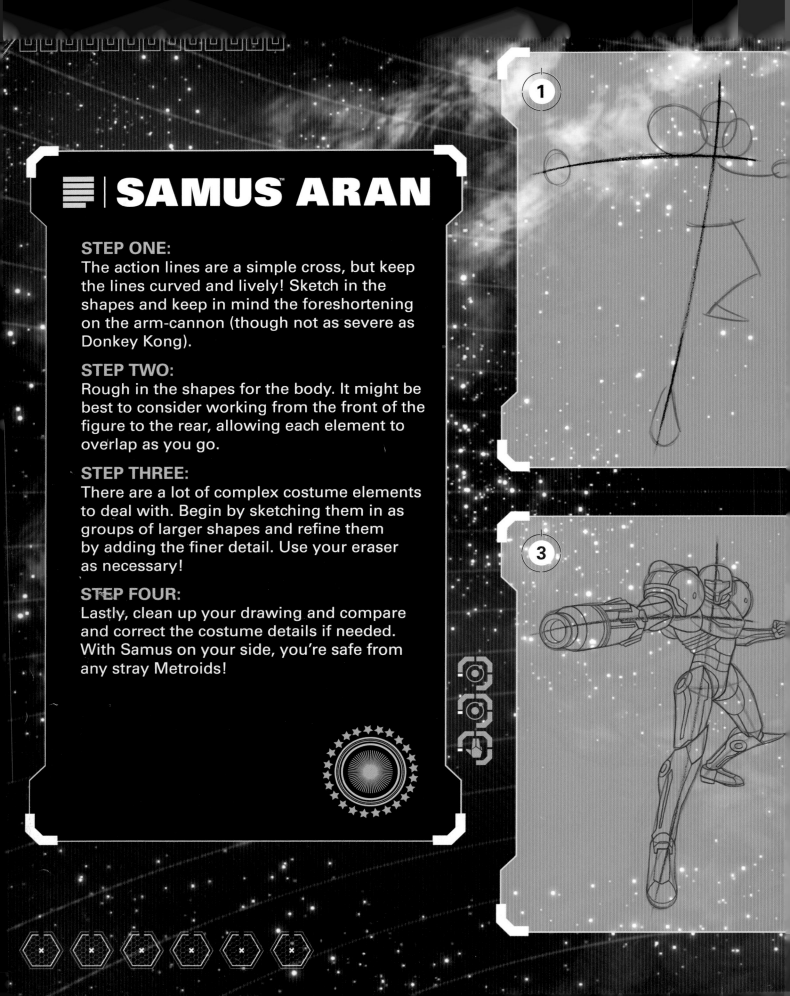

LINK™

STEP ONE:
Use a nice fluid curve for your action lines and place the other shapes as indicated to structure your sketch. The head crosshairs are important for placing the features later.

STEP TWO:
Rough in the shapes necessary to flesh out the figure. Notice how the body shapes mimic the flow of the action line you created. This will give your final drawing the appearance of movement.

STEP THREE:
Start by adding the facial features and then move on to the details of Link's costume and accessories. Some "stretch lines" in the fabric will help to accentuate the dynamics of the pose.

STEP FOUR:
Clean up the character sketch and fill in any details missed. If drawn correctly, our hero should look like he's caught in a brisk wind, with his hair flowing and his costume wafting.

PRINCESS ZELDA

1

2

3

4

STEP ONE:
After sketching in the action lines, add the basic shapes to build the figure. Because so much of her figure is covered in a gown, you can use large blocky shapes to rough in the drapery of the fabric.

STEP TWO:
Use the crosshairs to place the facial features and move on to roughing in the gown design. You can also place some of the jewelry shapes at this time.

STEP THREE:
The designs on Zelda's gown are intricate. Concentrate on the larger shapes that make up her figure and gown.

STEP FOUR:
Clean up the sketch as usual and carefully inspect your drawing for any details you may have overlooked. Don't worry if your gown designs don't perfectly match those of the example. Princesses are wonderfully forgiving, and I'm sure she'll look radiant in whatever you design!

CONGRATULATIONS!

You've now completed all the steps necessary to draw the most famous and beloved heroes and villains of all your favorite Nintendo games! So, now that you've mastered these poses, try drawing these characters in different poses or with different costumes. You can also consider adding backgrounds and even coloring your drawings! Whatever you decide, remember to follow the proper steps and to build your characters slowly.

And don't forget an artist's number one rule: **HAVE FUN!**

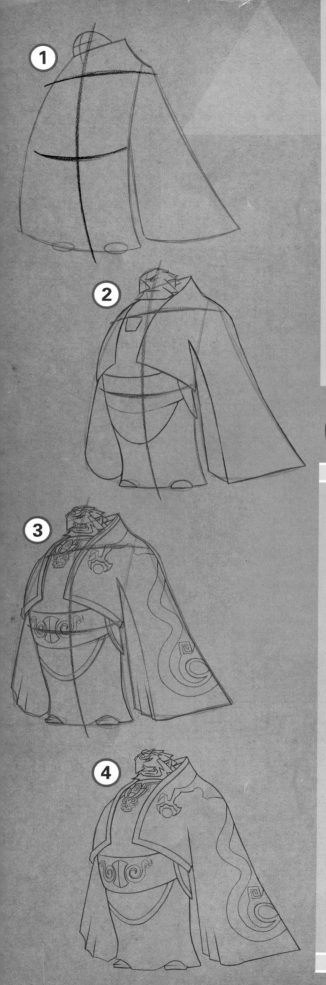

GANONDORF™

STEP ONE:
Just like the princess' pose, Ganondorf's shape is hidden beneath his robes. So, use your action lines and rough shapes to define the structure of his costume instead.

STEP TWO:
Sketch in the basic shapes to fill out Ganondorf's form. He's quite large, so keep a sense of volume in mind as you structure the character!

STEP THREE:
Sketch in the scowling features and then work on rendering the costume. Again, you might want to consider roughing in the more intricate designs on the robe for now and then tightening them up after the clean-up phase.

STEP FOUR:
Erase and strengthen to delineate your character's form and then work to mimic the complex designs that cover the robe … or make up your own!